THIS PLANNER

belongs to

AF269440

_____

SCHOOL

_____

GRADE_____   ROOM_____

ADDRESS_____

_____

EMAIL_____

PHONE_____

CONTACTS
and volunteers

NAME	CONTACT INFO

WELCOME

SCHEDULE

SCHOOL BEGINS: _____

LUNCH: _____ RECESS: _____

SPECIALS: _____

SCHOOL ENDS: _____

NEED HELP?

RELIABLE STUDENTS: _____

TEACHERS: _____

PRINCIPAL: _____

VICE PRINCIPAL: _____

OTHER STAFF: _____

SPECIAL SCHEDULES

NAME	TIME	LOCATION
_____	_____
_____	_____
_____	_____
_____	_____
_____	_____

ADDITIONAL NOTES

_____

_____

_____

_____

_____

_____

_____

COMMUNICATION LOG

DATE	TYPE	NAME	PURPOSE	NOTES
	📱 @ 📋 👥			
	📱 @ 📋 👥			
	📱 @ 📋 👥			
	📱 @ 📋 👥			
	📱 @ 📋 👥			
	📱 @ 📋 👥			
	📱 @ 📋 👥			
	📱 @ 📋 👥			
	📱 @ 📋 👥			
	📱 @ 📋 👥			
	📱 @ 📋 👥			
	📱 @ 📋 👥			
	📱 @ 📋 👥			
	📱 @ 📋 👥			
	📱 @ 📋 👥			
	📱 @ 📋 👥			
	📱 @ 📋 👥			
	📱 @ 📋 👥			
	📱 @ 📋 👥			
	📱 @ 📋 👥			
	📱 @ 📋 👥			
	📱 @ 📋 👥			
	📱 @ 📋 👥			
	📱 @ 📋 👥			
	📱 @ 📋 👥			
	📱 @ 📋 👥			

hello

COMMUNICATION LOG

DATE	TYPE	NAME	PURPOSE	NOTES
	📱 @ 📄 👥			
	📱 @ 📄 👥			
	📱 @ 📄 👥			
	📱 @ 📄 👥			
	📱 @ 📄 👥			
	📱 @ 📄 👥			
	📱 @ 📄 👥			
	📱 @ 📄 👥			
	📱 @ 📄 👥			
	📱 @ 📄 👥			
	📱 @ 📄 👥			
	📱 @ 📄 👥			
	📱 @ 📄 👥			
	📱 @ 📄 👥			
	📱 @ 📄 👥			
	📱 @ 📄 👥			
	📱 @ 📄 👥			
	📱 @ 📄 👥			
	📱 @ 📄 👥			
	📱 @ 📄 👥			
	📱 @ 📄 👥			
	📱 @ 📄 👥			
	📱 @ 📄 👥			
	📱 @ 📄 👥			
	📱 @ 📄 👥			
	📱 @ 📄 👥			
	📱 @ 📄 👥			

NEWS and Notes

GOOD VIBES

inhale, exhale

NEWS and Notes

BE STILL

I can Do hard things.

MAKE IT HAPPEN

PLAN IT ⚡

USE THESE PAGES TO CREATE A CLASSROOM PLAN, RECORD SEATING CHARTS, CREATE CHECKLISTS, SKETCH PLANS, ETC. THE OPTIONS ARE ENDLESS!

CHOOSE HAPPY.

Year at a GLANCE

JULY

AUGUST

SEPTEMBER

OCTOBER

NOVEMBER

DECEMBER

Year at a GLANCE

JANUARY

FEBRUARY

MARCH

APRIL

MAY

JUNE

JULY

MAKIN' A DIFFERENCE, DAILY.

SUNDAY	MONDAY	TUESDAY	WEDNESDAY

GOALS

THURSDAY	FRIDAY	SATURDAY	HAVE TO DO
○	○	○	○ _____ ○ _____ ○ _____ ○ _____ ○ _____ ○ _____ ○ _____ ○ _____ ○ _____ ○ _____ ○ _____ ○ _____ ○ _____
○	○	○	
○	○	○	NOTES
○	○	○	
○	○	○	

AUGUST

PAUSE. BREATHE. YOU'VE GOT THIS.

SUNDAY	MONDAY	TUESDAY	WEDNESDAY

GOALS

THURSDAY	FRIDAY	SATURDAY	HAVE TO DO
			NOTES

SEPTEMBER

NEVER STOP LEARNING.

SUNDAY	MONDAY	TUESDAY	WEDNESDAY

THURSDAY	FRIDAY	SATURDAY	HAVE TO DO
			NOTES

OCTOBER

TEACH YOUR HEART OUT.

SUNDAY	MONDAY	TUESDAY	WEDNESDAY

THURSDAY	FRIDAY	SATURDAY	HAVE TO DO
			○
			○
			○
			○
			○
			○
			○
			○
			○
			○
			○
			○
			NOTES

IMPORTANT DATES

GOALS

NOVEMBER

TEACHERS GONNA TEACH.

SUNDAY	MONDAY	TUESDAY	WEDNESDAY

THURSDAY	FRIDAY	SATURDAY	HAVE TO DO
			NOTES

DECEMBER

MAY YOUR COFFEE BE STRONG AND YOUR STUDENTS BE CALM.

SUNDAY	MONDAY	TUESDAY	WEDNESDAY

22

THURSDAY	FRIDAY	SATURDAY	HAVE TO DO
			NOTES

JANUARY

TEACH, GRADE, REPEAT.

SUNDAY	MONDAY	TUESDAY	WEDNESDAY

THURSDAY	FRIDAY	SATURDAY	HAVE TO DO
			NOTES

FEBRUARY

KEEP CALM, IT'S ON THE LESSON PLAN.

SUNDAY	MONDAY	TUESDAY	WEDNESDAY

IMPORTANT DATES

GOALS

THURSDAY	FRIDAY	SATURDAY	HAVE TO DO
			○
			○
			○
			○
			○
			○
			○
			○
			○
			○
			○
			○
			NOTES

MARCH

LET CURIOSITY LEAD THE WAY.

SUNDAY	MONDAY	TUESDAY	WEDNESDAY

THURSDAY	FRIDAY	SATURDAY	HAVE TO DO
			NOTES

29

APRIL

GIVE THEM SOMETHING GREAT TO IMITATE.

SUNDAY	MONDAY	TUESDAY	WEDNESDAY

30

GOALS

THURSDAY	FRIDAY	SATURDAY	HAVE TO DO

NOTES

MAY

TEACHERS HAVE CLASS.

SUNDAY	MONDAY	TUESDAY	WEDNESDAY

THURSDAY	FRIDAY	SATURDAY	HAVE TO DO
			NOTES

JUNE

MESSY CLASSROOMS ARE WHERE THE FUN STUFF HAPPENS.

SUNDAY	MONDAY	TUESDAY	WEDNESDAY

THURSDAY	FRIDAY	SATURDAY	HAVE TO DO
			NOTES

SUBJECT	SUBJECT	SUBJECT

MON.
/

TUES.
/

WED.
/

THURS.
/

FRI.
/

SUBJECT	SUBJECT	SUBJECT

SUBJECT	SUBJECT	SUBJECT	SUBJECT

PSST! CUT OFF THIS CORNER EACH WEEK TO MARK AND FIND YOUR PLACE EASILY.

SUBJECT	SUBJECT	SUBJECT

MON.
/

TUES.
/

WED.
/

THURS.
/

FRI.
/

SUBJECT	SUBJECT	SUBJECT	SUBJECT

39

SUBJECT	SUBJECT	SUBJECT

MON.
/

TUES.
/

WED.
/

THURS.
/

FRI.
/

SUBJECT	SUBJECT	SUBJECT	SUBJECT

SUBJECT	SUBJECT	SUBJECT

MON.

/

TUES.

/

WED.

/

THURS.

/

FRI.

/

SUBJECT	SUBJECT	SUBJECT	SUBJECT

SUBJECT	SUBJECT	SUBJECT

MON. /

TUES. /

WED. /

THURS. /

FRI. /

SUBJECT	SUBJECT	SUBJECT	SUBJECT

SUBJECT	SUBJECT	SUBJECT

MON.
/

TUES.
/

WED.
/

THURS.
/

FRI.
/

SUBJECT	SUBJECT	SUBJECT	SUBJECT

WEEK #

SUBJECT	SUBJECT	SUBJECT

MON.
/

TUES.
/

WED.
/

THURS.
/

FRI.
/

48

SUBJECT	SUBJECT	SUBJECT	SUBJECT

	SUBJECT	SUBJECT	SUBJECT
MON. /			
TUES. /			
WED. /			
THURS. /			
FRI. /			

SUBJECT	SUBJECT	SUBJECT	SUBJECT

	SUBJECT	SUBJECT	SUBJECT
MON. /			
TUES. /			
WED. /			
THURS. /			
FRI. /			

SUBJECT	SUBJECT	SUBJECT	SUBJECT

SUBJECT	SUBJECT	SUBJECT

MON.

/

TUES.

/

WED.

/

THURS.

/

FRI.

/

SUBJECT	SUBJECT	SUBJECT	SUBJECT

SUBJECT	SUBJECT	SUBJECT

MON.
/

TUES.
/

WED.
/

THURS.
/

FRI.
/

SUBJECT	SUBJECT	SUBJECT	SUBJECT

SUBJECT	SUBJECT	SUBJECT

MON.
/

TUES.
/

WED.
/

THURS.
/

FRI.
/

SUBJECT	SUBJECT	SUBJECT	SUBJECT

SUBJECT	SUBJECT	SUBJECT

MON.
/

TUES.
/

WED.
/

THURS.
/

FRI.
/

SUBJECT	SUBJECT	SUBJECT	SUBJECT

SUBJECT	SUBJECT	SUBJECT

MON.
/

TUES.
/

WED.
/

THURS.
/

FRI.
/

SUBJECT	SUBJECT	SUBJECT	SUBJECT

WEEK

SUBJECT	SUBJECT	SUBJECT

MON.
/

TUES.
/

WED.
/

THURS.
/

FRI.
/

SUBJECT	SUBJECT	SUBJECT	SUBJECT

SUBJECT	SUBJECT	SUBJECT

MON.
/

TUES.
/

WED.
/

THURS.
/

FRI.
/

SUBJECT	SUBJECT	SUBJECT	SUBJECT

WEEK#	SUBJECT	SUBJECT	SUBJECT
MON. /			
TUES. /			
WED. /			
THURS. /			
FRI. /			

SUBJECT	SUBJECT	SUBJECT	SUBJECT

WEEK

SUBJECT	SUBJECT	SUBJECT

MON. /

TUES. /

WED. /

THURS. /

FRI. /

SUBJECT	SUBJECT	SUBJECT	SUBJECT

SUBJECT	SUBJECT	SUBJECT

MON.

/

TUES.

/

WED.

/

THURS.

/

FRI.

/

SUBJECT	SUBJECT	SUBJECT	SUBJECT

SUBJECT	SUBJECT	SUBJECT

MON.
/

TUES.
/

WED.
/

THURS.
/

FRI.
/

SUBJECT	SUBJECT	SUBJECT	SUBJECT

	SUBJECT	SUBJECT	SUBJECT
MON. /			
TUES. /			
WED. /			
THURS. /			
FRI. /			

SUBJECT	SUBJECT	SUBJECT	SUBJECT

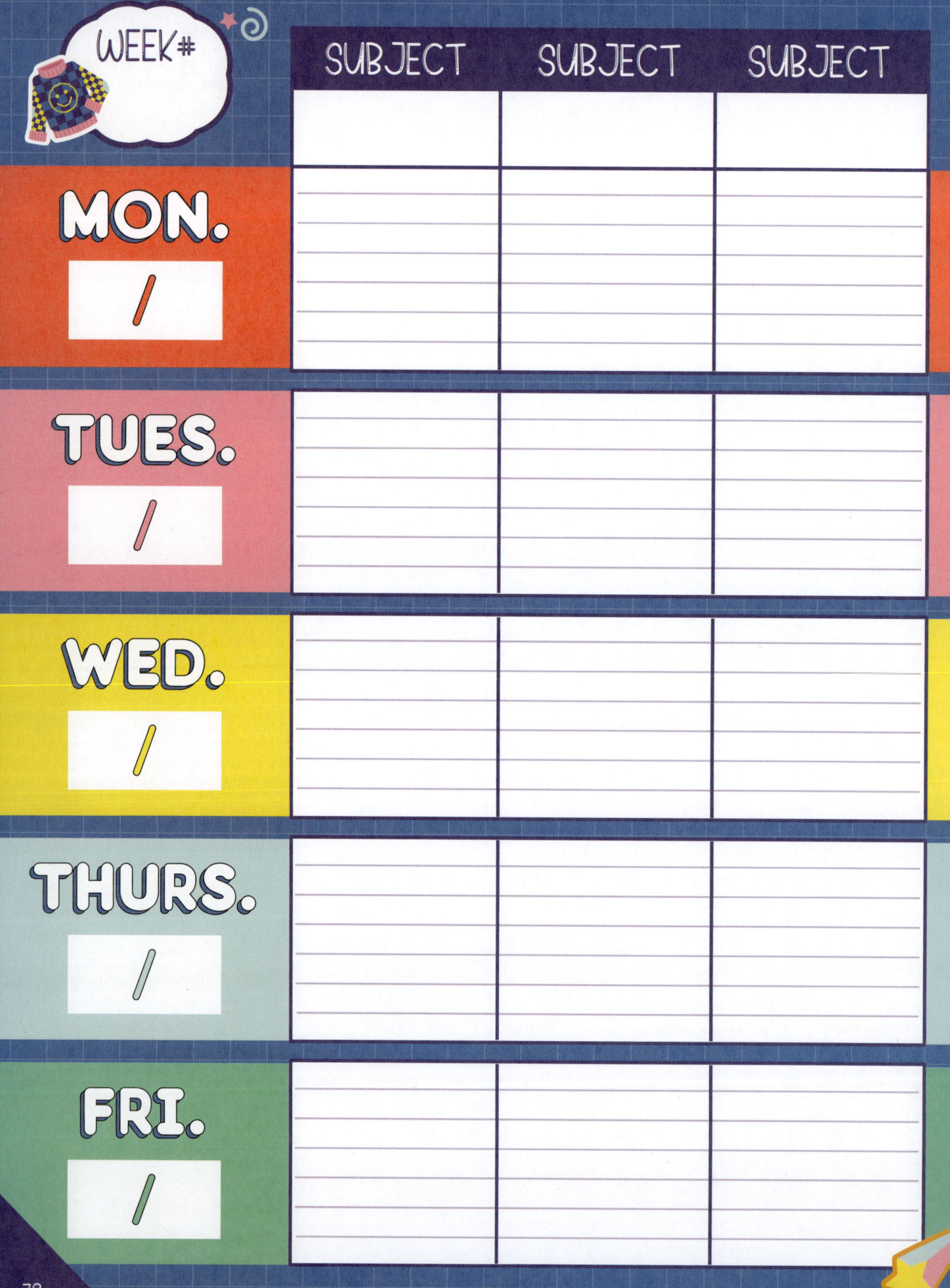

WEEK#

SUBJECT	SUBJECT	SUBJECT

MON. /

TUES. /

WED. /

THURS. /

FRI. /

SUBJECT	SUBJECT	SUBJECT	SUBJECT

WEEK#

SUBJECT	SUBJECT	SUBJECT

MON.
/

TUES.
/

WED.
/

THURS.
/

FRI.
/

SUBJECT	SUBJECT	SUBJECT	SUBJECT

WEEK#

SUBJECT	SUBJECT	SUBJECT

MON.
/

TUES.
/

WED.
/

THURS.
/

FRI.
/

82

SUBJECT	SUBJECT	SUBJECT	SUBJECT

	SUBJECT	SUBJECT	SUBJECT
WEEK#			
MON. /			
TUES. /			
WED. /			
THURS. /			
FRI. /			

84

SUBJECT	SUBJECT	SUBJECT	SUBJECT

SUBJECT	SUBJECT	SUBJECT

MON.

/

TUES.

/

WED.

/

THURS.

/

FRI.

/

SUBJECT	SUBJECT	SUBJECT	SUBJECT

SUBJECT	SUBJECT	SUBJECT

MON.
/

TUES.
/

WED.
/

THURS.
/

FRI.
/

SUBJECT	SUBJECT	SUBJECT	SUBJECT

SUBJECT	SUBJECT	SUBJECT

MON.
/

TUES.
/

WED.
/

THURS.
/

FRI.
/

SUBJECT	SUBJECT	SUBJECT	SUBJECT

SUBJECT	SUBJECT	SUBJECT

MON.

/

TUES.

/

WED.

/

THURS.

/

FRI.

/

SUBJECT	SUBJECT	SUBJECT	SUBJECT

SUBJECT	SUBJECT	SUBJECT

MON. /

TUES. /

WED. /

THURS. /

FRI. /

SUBJECT	SUBJECT	SUBJECT	SUBJECT

SUBJECT	SUBJECT	SUBJECT

MON.
/

TUES.
/

WED.
/

THURS.
/

FRI.
/

SUBJECT	SUBJECT	SUBJECT	SUBJECT

SUBJECT	SUBJECT	SUBJECT

MON.
/

TUES.
/

WED.
/

THURS.
/

FRI.
/

SUBJECT	SUBJECT	SUBJECT	SUBJECT

WEEK

SUBJECT	SUBJECT	SUBJECT

MON.
/

TUES.
/

WED.
/

THURS.
/

FRI.
/

SUBJECT	SUBJECT	SUBJECT	SUBJECT

	SUBJECT	SUBJECT	SUBJECT
MON. /			
TUES. /			
WED. /			
THURS. /			
FRI. /			

SUBJECT	SUBJECT	SUBJECT	SUBJECT

SUBJECT	SUBJECT	SUBJECT

MON.
/

TUES.
/

WED.
/

THURS.
/

FRI.
/

SUBJECT	SUBJECT	SUBJECT	SUBJECT

SUBJECT	SUBJECT	SUBJECT

MON.
/

TUES.
/

WED.
/

THURS.
/

FRI.
/

SUBJECT	SUBJECT	SUBJECT	SUBJECT

WEEK #

SUBJECT	SUBJECT	SUBJECT

MON.
/

TUES.
/

WED.
/

THURS.
/

FRI.
/

SUBJECT	SUBJECT	SUBJECT	SUBJECT

SUBJECT	SUBJECT	SUBJECT

MON.
/

TUES.
/

WED.
/

THURS.
/

FRI.
/

SUBJECT	SUBJECT	SUBJECT	SUBJECT

SUBJECT	SUBJECT	SUBJECT

MON.
/

TUES.
/

WED.
/

THURS.
/

FRI.
/

SUBJECT	SUBJECT	SUBJECT	SUBJECT

SUBJECT	SUBJECT	SUBJECT

MON. /

TUES. /

WED. /

THURS. /

FRI. /

SUBJECT	SUBJECT	SUBJECT	SUBJECT

STUDENT CHECKLIST

NAME

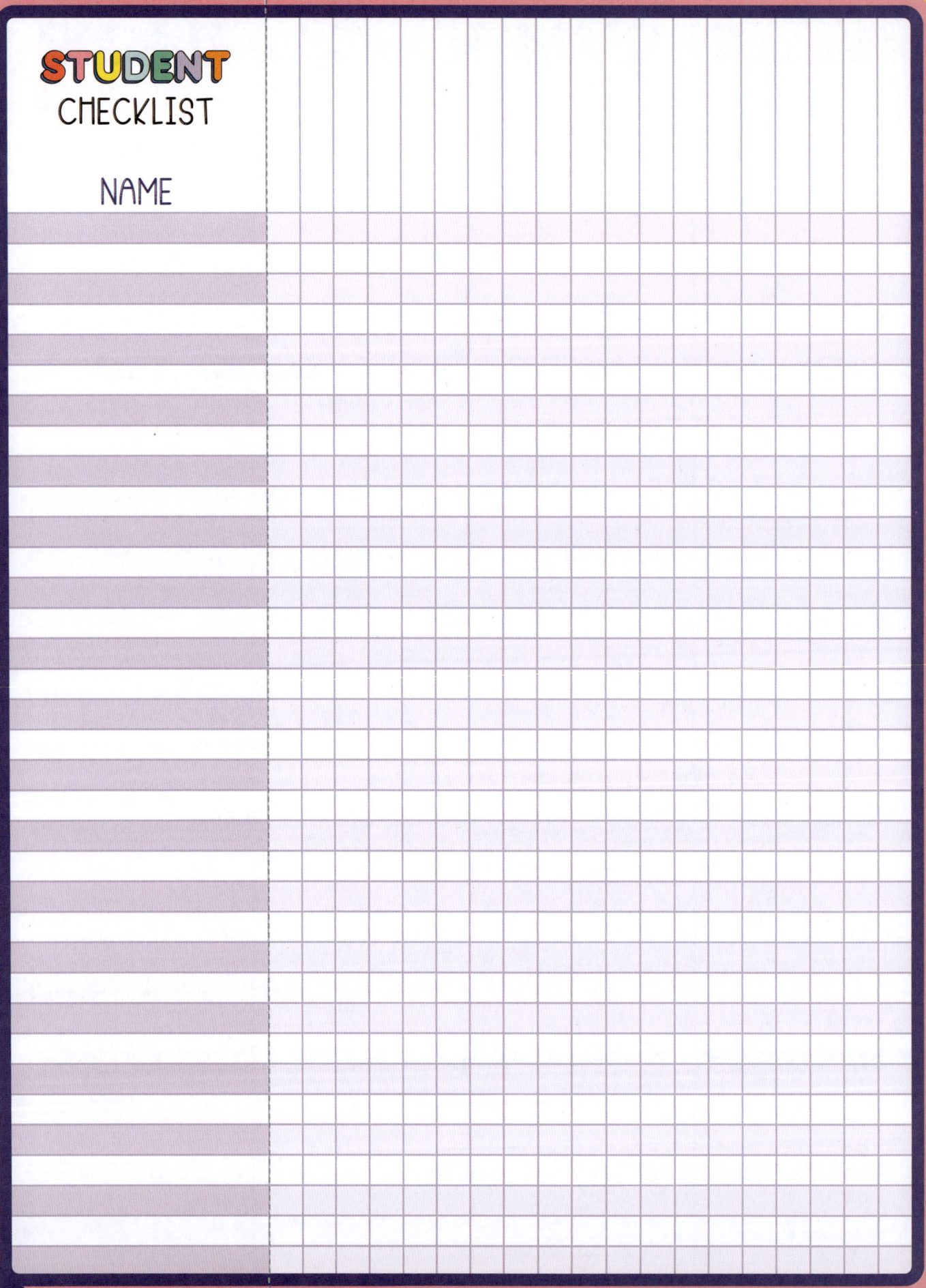

STUDENT CHECKLIST

NAME

PSST! CUT OFF THIS SECTION SO THAT YOU ONLY HAVE TO WRITE YOUR CLASS LIST ONCE.

118

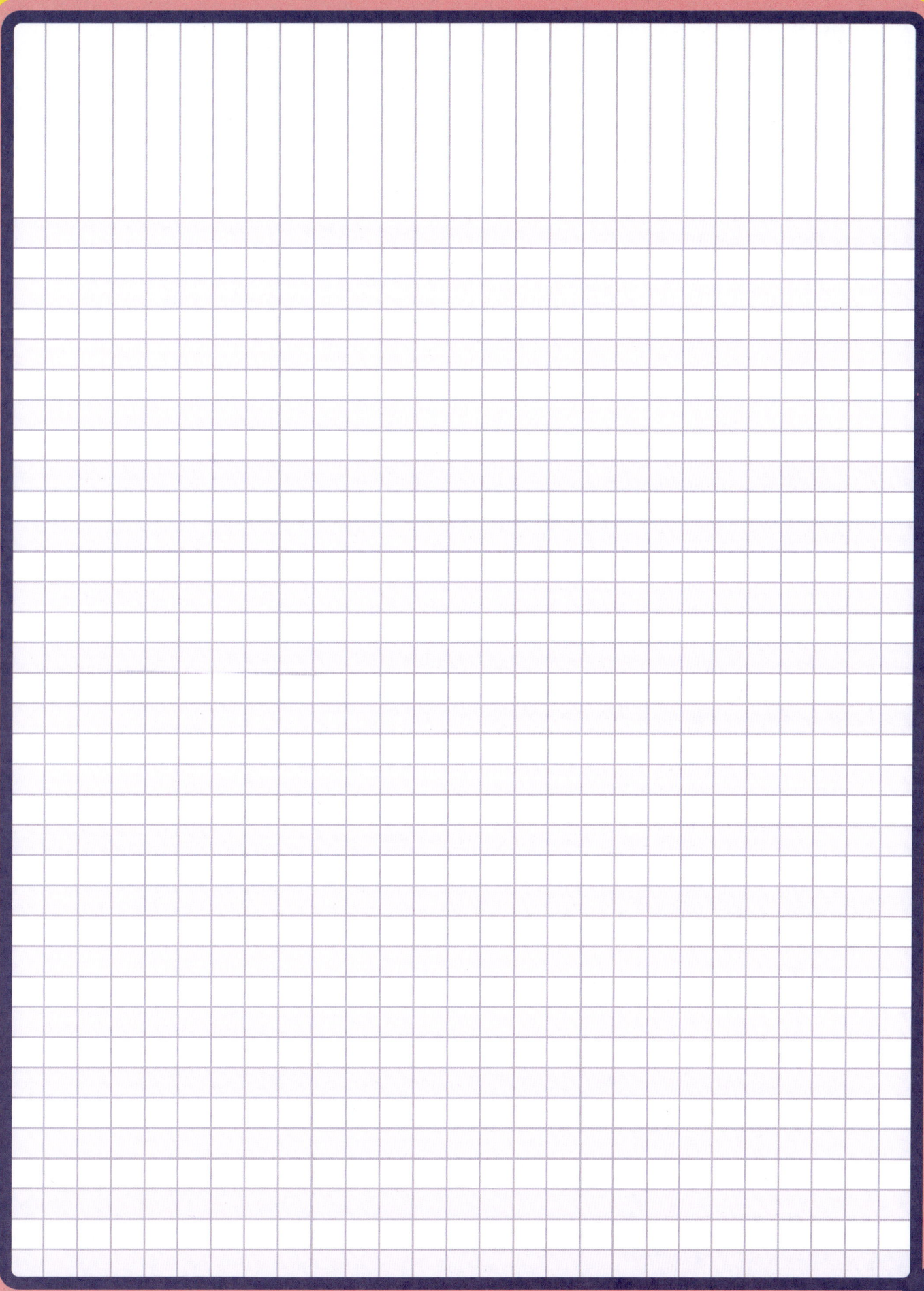

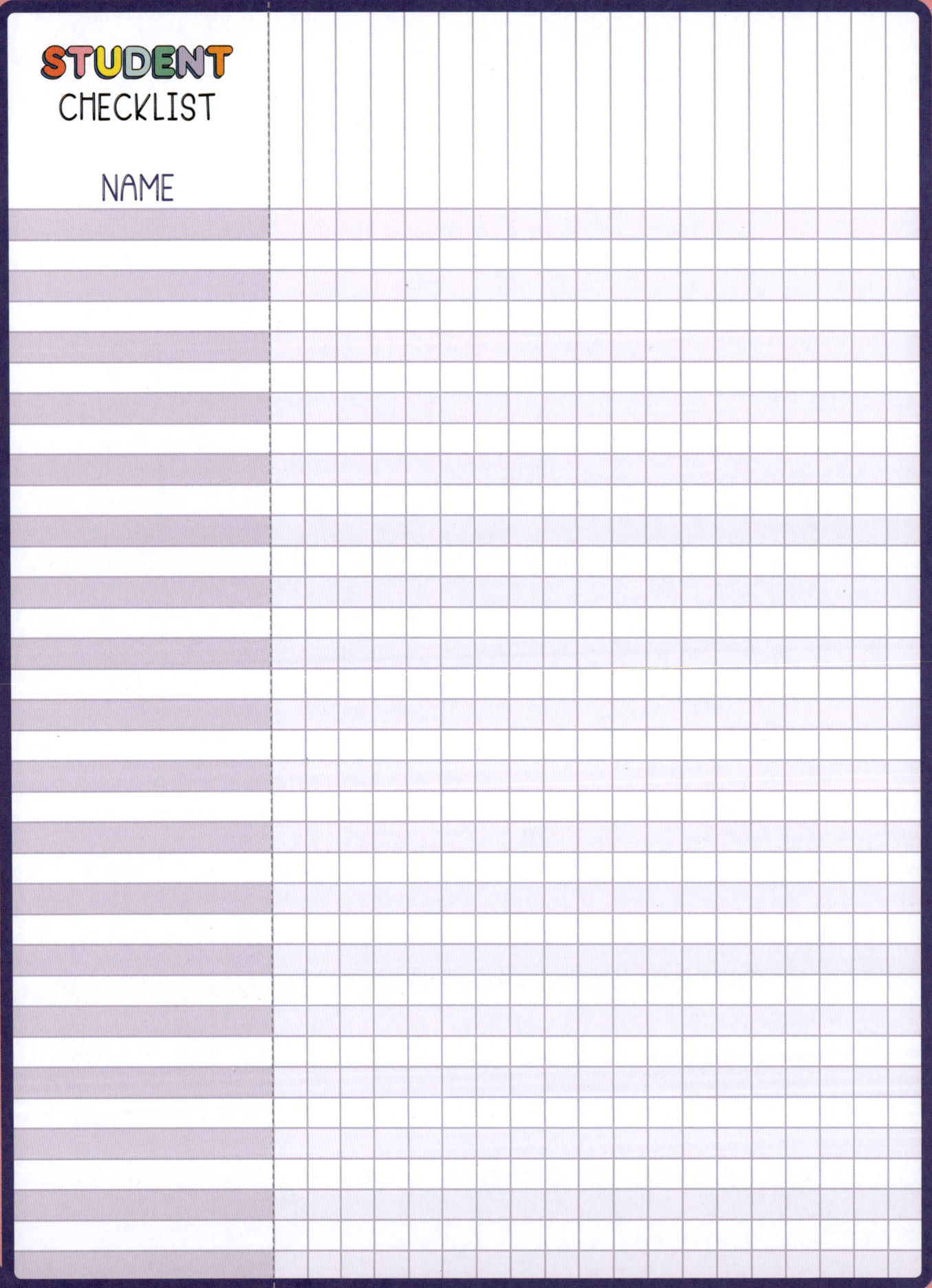

STUDENT
CHECKLIST

NAME

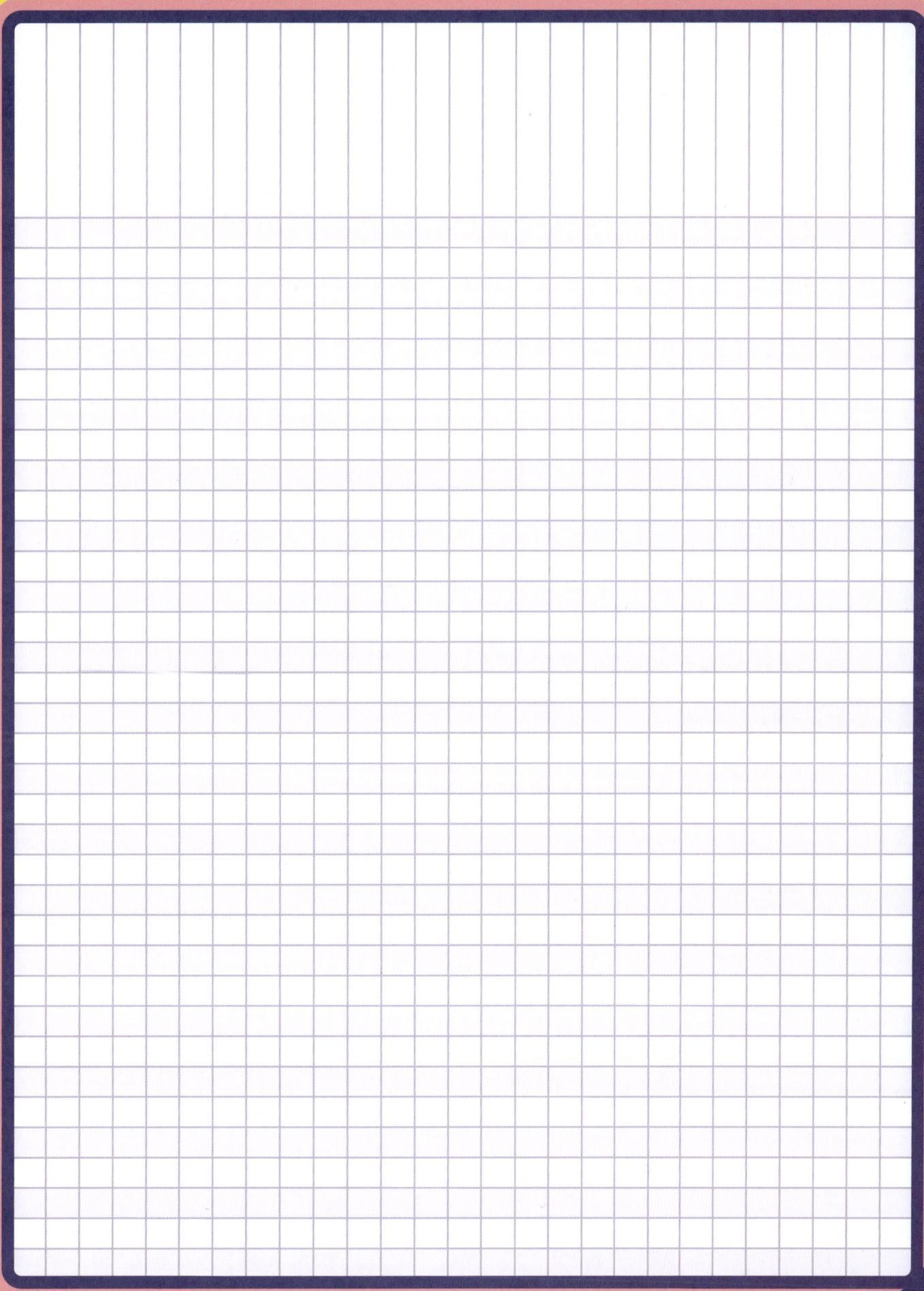

STUDENT
CHECKLIST

NAME

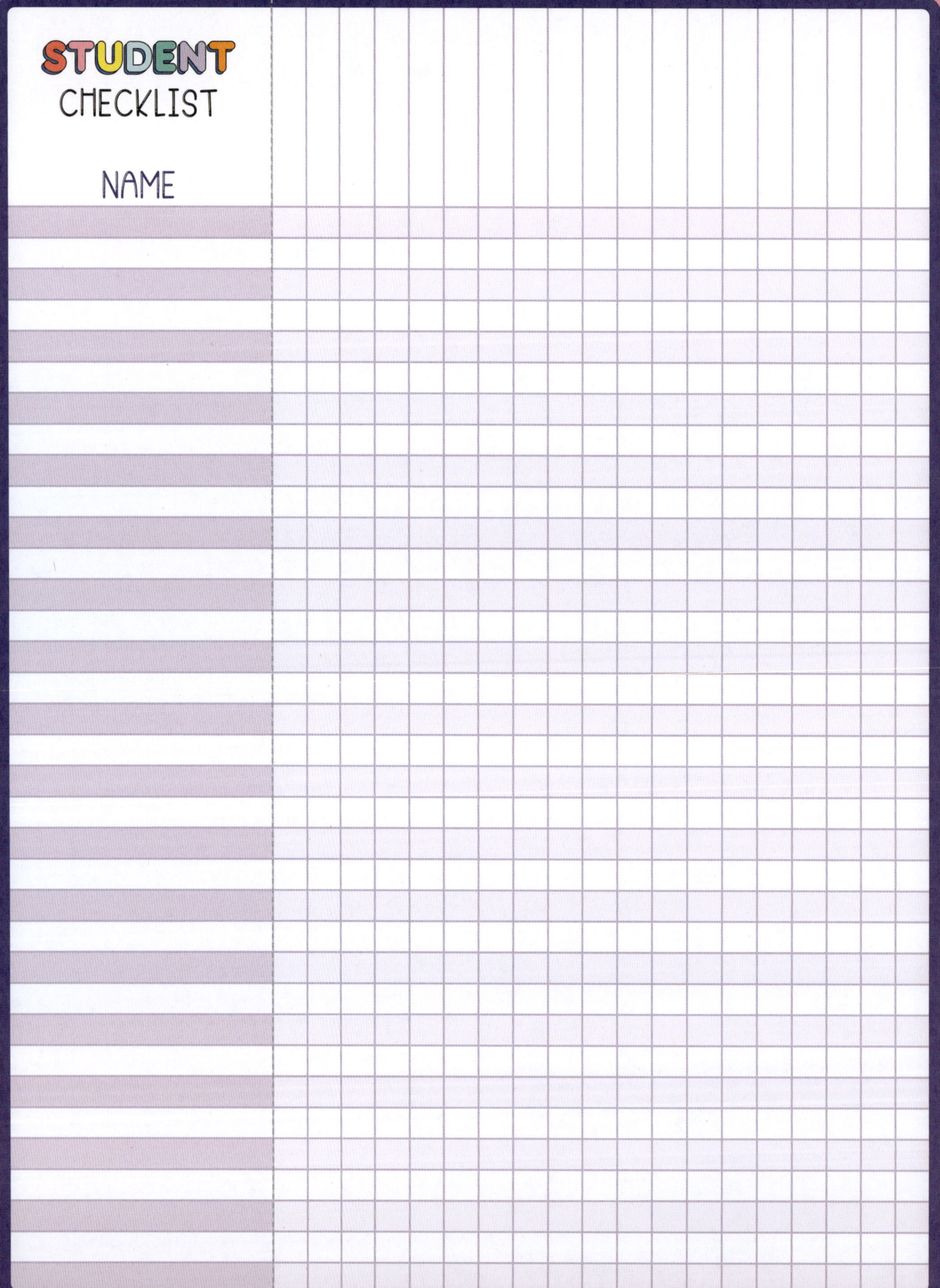

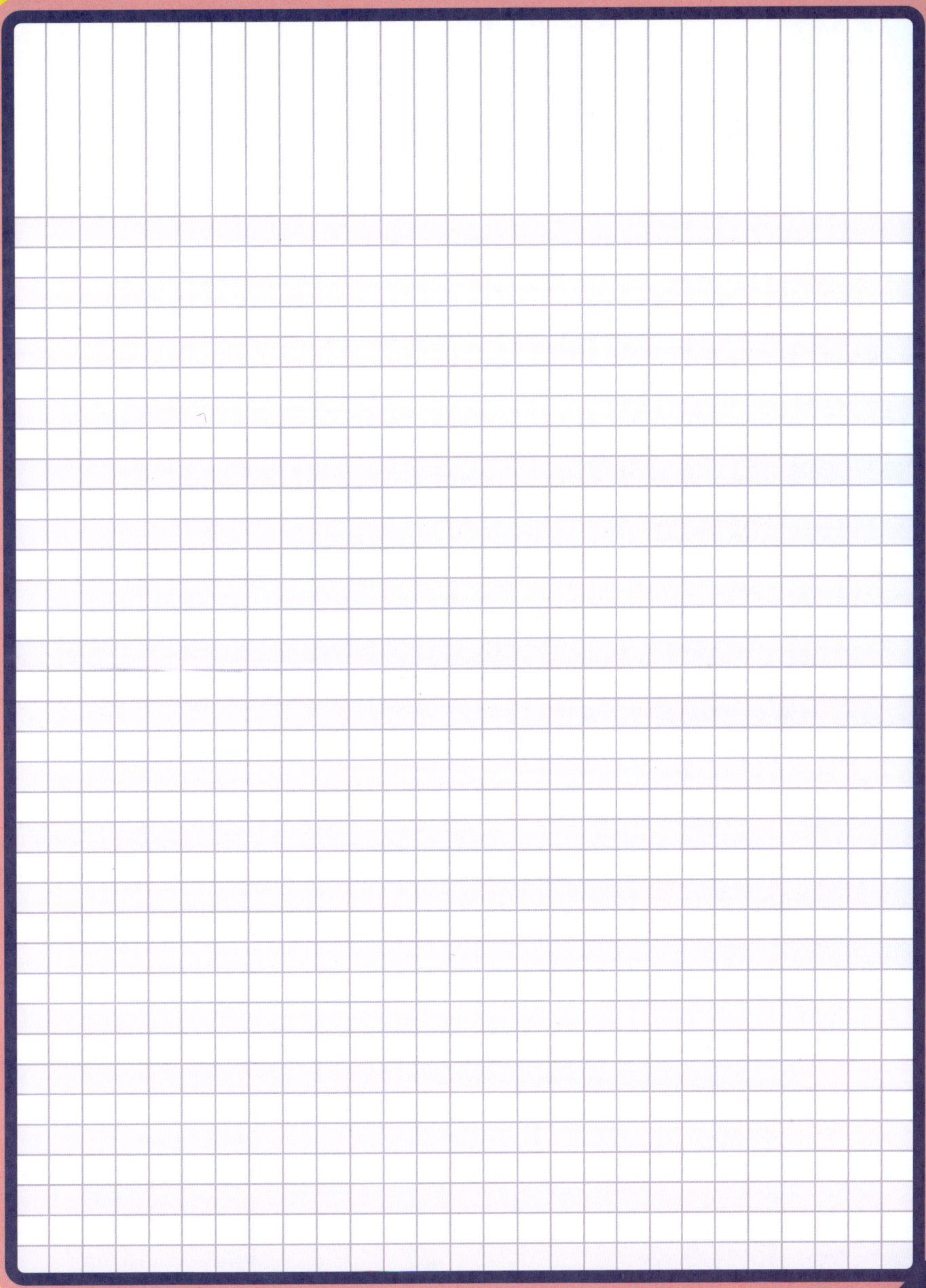

STUDENT
CHECKLIST

NAME

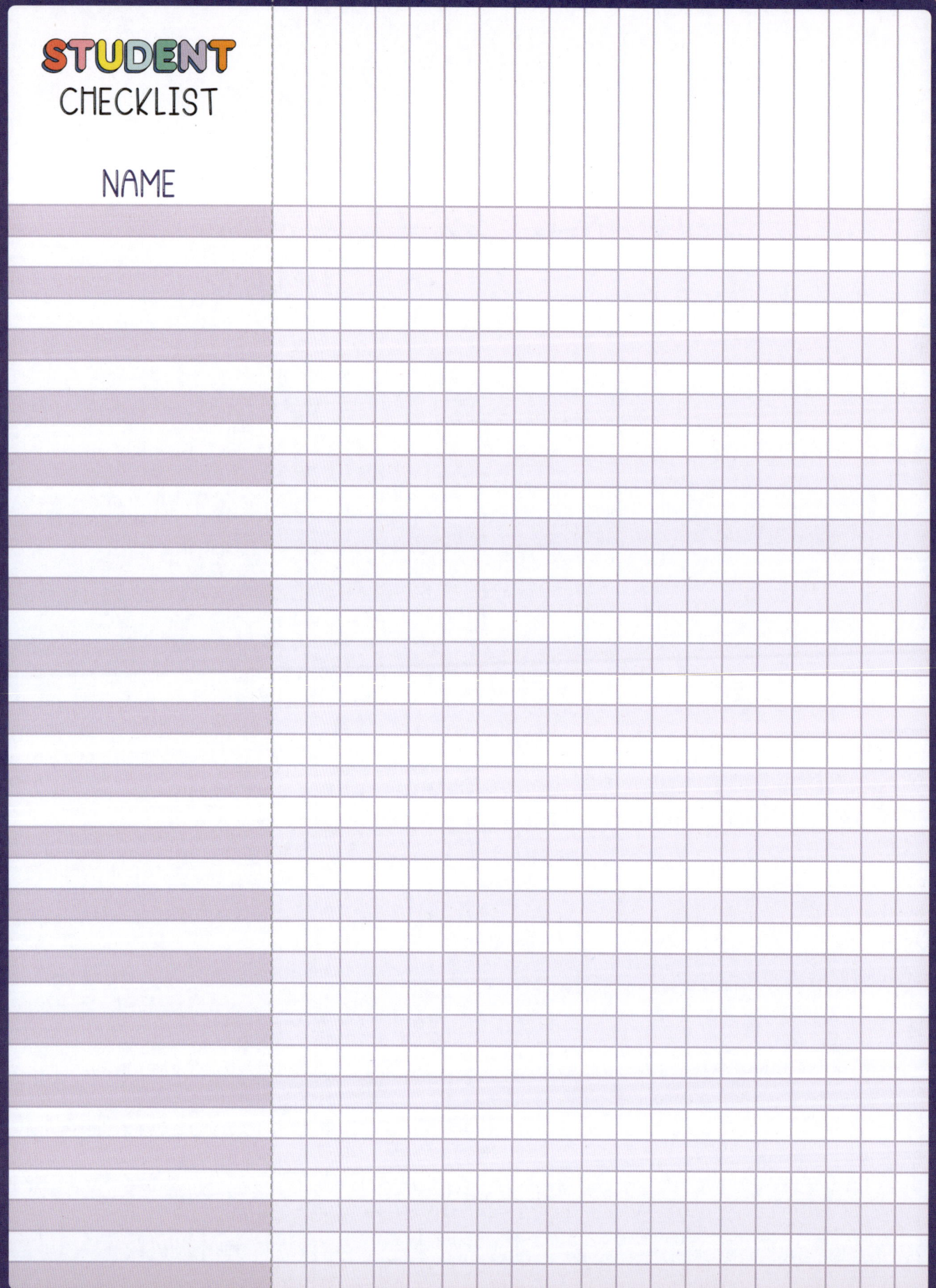

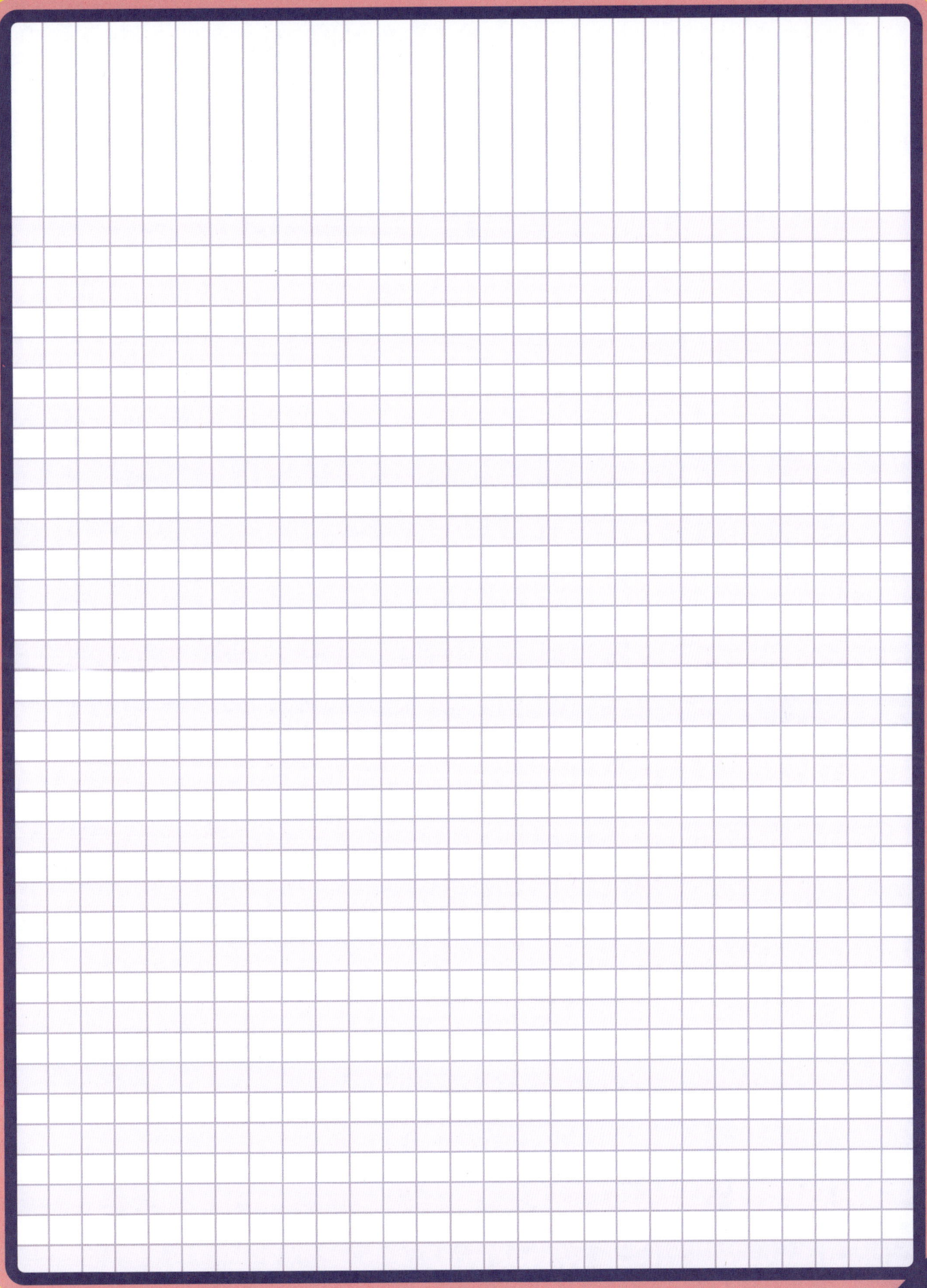

STUDENT CHECKLIST

NAME

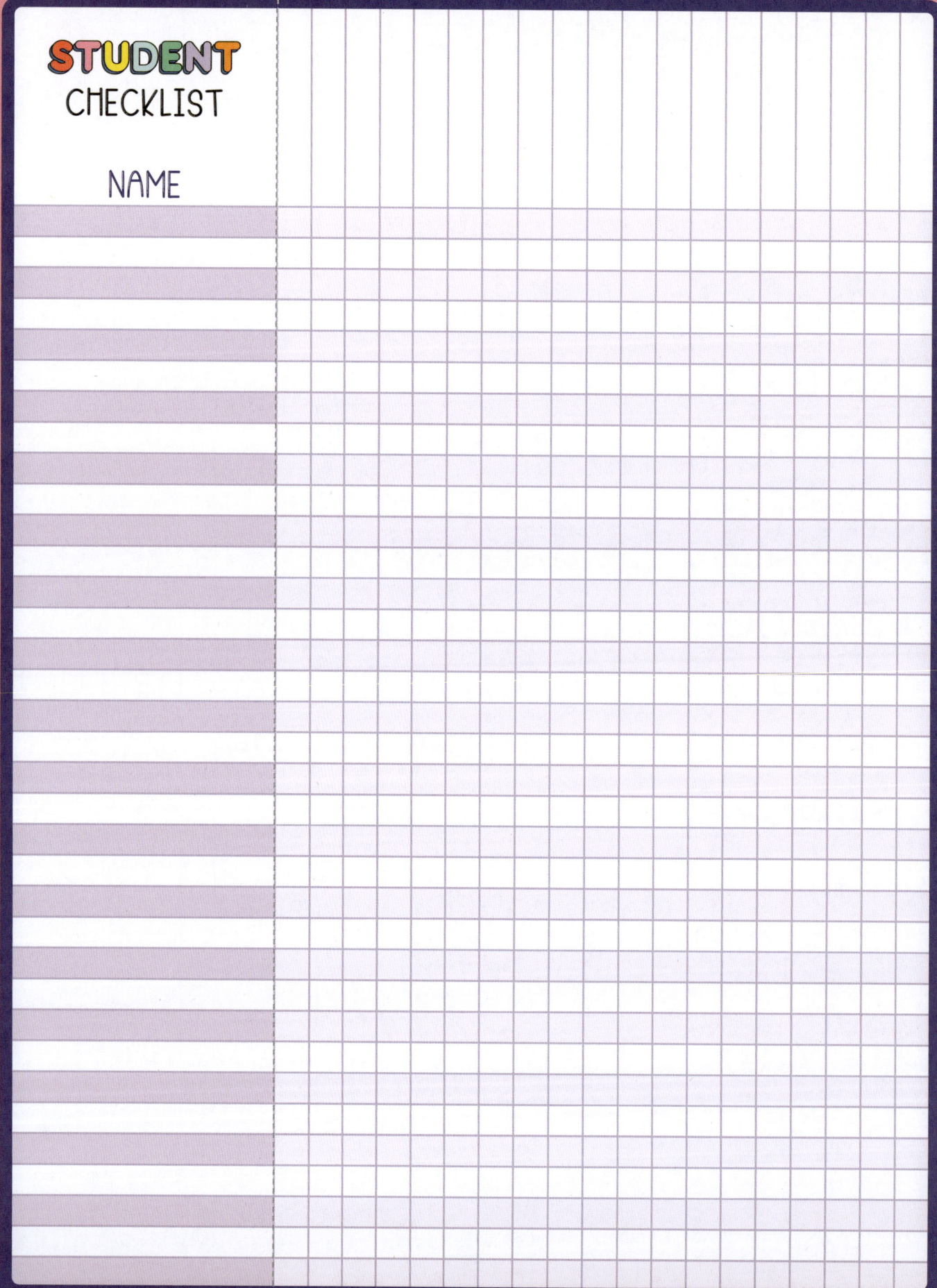

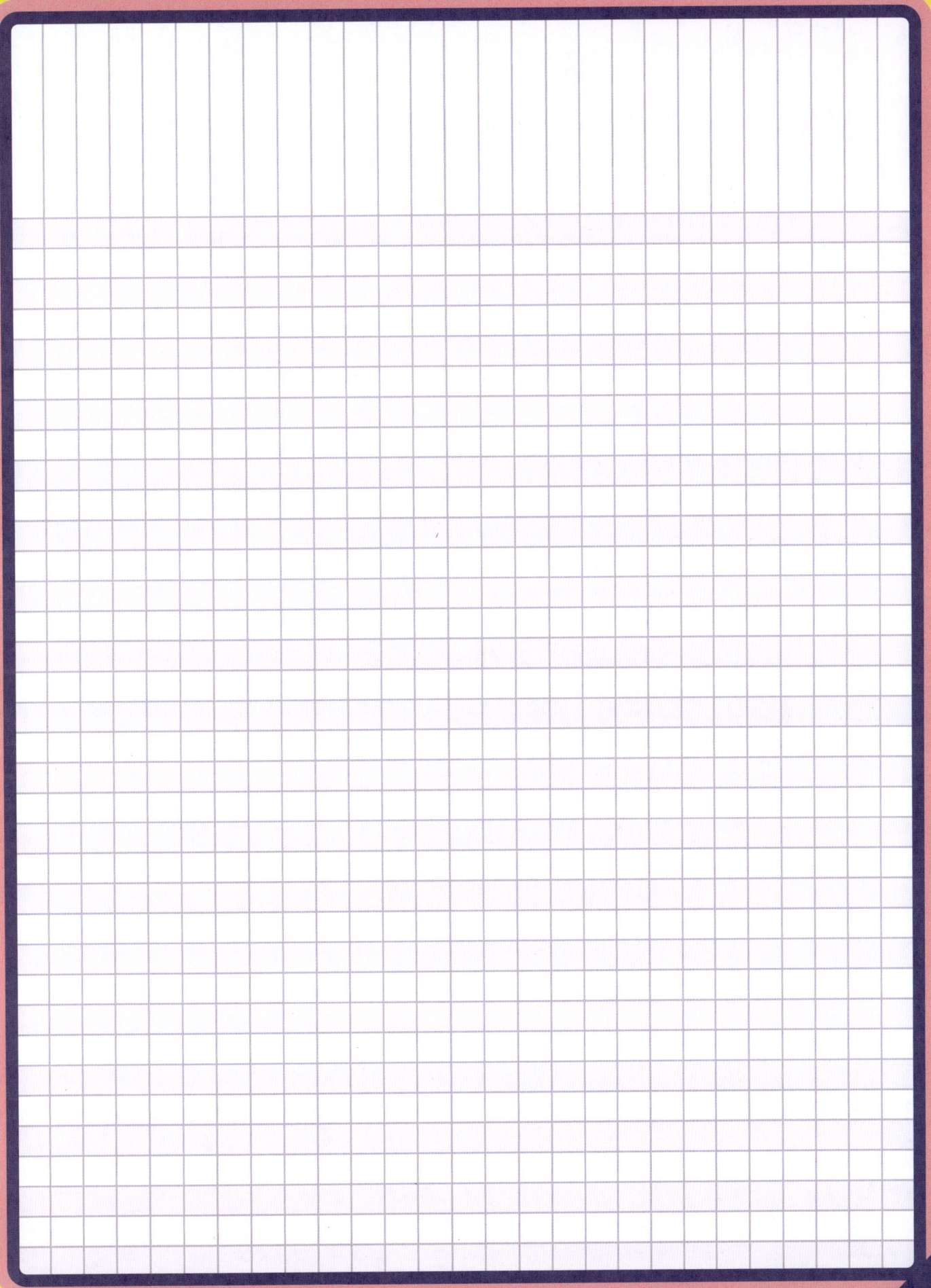

JULY JULY

AUGUST AUGUST

SEPTEMBER SEPTEMBER

OCTOBER OCTOBER

NOVEMBER NOVEMBER

DECEMBER DECEMBER

JANUARY JANUARY

FEBRUARY FEBRUARY

MARCH MARCH

APRIL APRIL

MAY MAY

JUNE JUNE

CHECKLISTS CHECKLISTS

LESSON PLANS LESSON PLANS

CONFERENCES	CONFERENCES	STAFF MEETING	STAFF MEETING	PROFESSIONAL DEV.
CONFERENCES	CONFERENCES	STAFF MEETING	STAFF MEETING	
ASSEMBLY	EARLY RELEASE	EARLY RELEASE	EARLY RELEASE	
ASSEMBLY	EARLY RELEASE	EARLY RELEASE	EARLY RELEASE	PROFESSIONAL DEV.
HOLIDAY	HOLIDAY	HOLIDAY	TESTING	
HOLIDAY	HOLIDAY	HOLIDAY	TESTING	
NO SCHOOL	NO SCHOOL	NO SCHOOL	iEP MEETING	PROFESSIONAL DEV.
NO SCHOOL	NO SCHOOL	NO SCHOOL	iEP MEETING	
REPORT CARDS	REPORT CARDS	REPORT CARDS	REPORT CARDS	

*TAKE NOTE

*PRIORITY

FIELD TRIP

REMEMBER!	REMEMBER!
REMEMBER!	REMEMBER!
MUST DO!	MUST DO!
MUST DO!	MUST DO!

FIELD TRIP

FIELD TRIP

*DON'T FORGET

*TODAY

| DO THIS! | DO THIS! |
| DO THIS! | DO THIS! |

PROGRESS REPORTS

| DUE | DUE |

PROGRESS REPORTS

*GET IT DONE!

*BUSY DAY

PROGRESS REPORTS

| DUE | DUE |
| DUE | DUE |

PROGRESS REPORTS